KU-198-770

ANTIQUES AND THEIR VALUES

CLOCKS & WATCHES

COMPILED BY TONY CURTIS

While every care has been taken in the compiling of information contained in this volume the publishers cannot accept any liability for loss, financial or otherwise, incurred by reliance placed on the information herein.

All prices quoted in this book are obtained from a variety of auctions in various countries and are converted to dollars at the rate of exchange prevalent at the time of sale.

ISBN   0-86248-010-8

Copyright © Lyle Publications MCMLXXXI
Published by Lyle Publications, Glenmayne, Galashiels, Selkirkshire, Scotland.

INTRODUCTION

This book is one of a series specially devised to aid the busy professional dealer in his everyday trading. It will also prove to be of great value to all collectors and those with goods to sell, for it is crammed with illustrations, brief descriptions and valuations of hundreds of antiques.

Every effort has been made to ensure that each specialised volume contains the widest possible variety of goods in its particular category though the greatest emphasis is placed on the middle bracket of trade goods rather than on those once-in-a-lifetime museum pieces whose values are of academic rather than practical interest to the vast majority of dealers and collectors.

This policy has been followed as a direct consequence of requests from dealers who sensibly realise that, no matter how comprehensive their knowledge, there is always a need for reliable, up-to-date reference works for identification and valuation purposes.

When using your Antiques and their Values Book to assess the worth of goods, please bear in mind that it would be impossible to place upon any item a precise value which would hold good under all circumstances. No antique has an exactly calculable value; its price is always the result of a compromise reached between buyer and seller, and questions of condition, local demand and the business acumen of the parties involved in a sale are all factors which affect the assessment of an object's 'worth' in terms of hard cash.

In the final analysis, however, such factors cancel out when large numbers of sales are taken into account by an experienced valuer, and it is possible to arrive at a surprisingly accurate assessment of current values of antiques; an assessment which may be taken confidently to be a fair indication of the worth of an object and which provides a reliable basis for negotiation.

Throughout this book, objects are grouped under category headings and, to expedite reference, they progress in price order within their own categories. Where the description states 'one of a pair' the value given is that for the pair sold as such.

The publishers wish to express their sincere thanks
to the following for their kind help and assistance
in the production of this volume:

JANICE MONCRIEFF
NICOLA PARK
CARMEN MILIVOYEVICH
ELAINE HARLAND
MAY MUTCH
MARGOT RUTHERFORD
JENNIFER KNOX

Printed by Apollo Press, Worthing, Sussex, England.
Bound by R. J. Acford, Chichester, Sussex, England.

CONTENTS

BRACKET CLOCKS

Edwardian mahogany bracket clock with inlaid stringing. $250   £110

Ornate French bracket clock with ormolu decoration.$330 £145

19th century bracket clock, 14in. high, in mahogany and brass case. $330 £145

Quarter repeating oak bracket clock, circa 1900, 16in. high.
$370 £165

Mahogany bracket clock by F. J. Dent, London, 18in. high, circa 1840.
$520 £230

A George IV mahogany bracket clock, 1ft.3½in. high. $980 £435

German oak bracket clock, circa 1890, 21½in. high.
$1,000 £450

Bracket clock by Henning of Lymington.
$1,070 £475

Early 19th century bracket clock by J. Harper, London.
$1,080 £480

William IV mahogany
bracket clock, dial
inscribed Taylor & Son,
Bristol, 19in. high.
$1,150 £510

Regency ebonised striking
bracket clock, signed
Moncas, Liverpool, 18½in.
high. $1,215 £540

Mahogany bracket clock
by W. Robson, N. Shields,
46cm. high. $1,240 £550

George III mahogany brac-
ket clock by William
Cozens of London, 1ft.
3½in. tall. $1,285 £570

Late Victorian mahogany
bracket clock signed A. &
M. Rowley, London,
25in. high. $1,285 £570

Early 19th century ebon-
ised lancet top bracket
clock by Grant, London.
$1,300 £580

Early 19th century bracket
clock by P. Grimalde.
$1,350 £600

Oak bracket clock, dial
signed Clerke 1, London,
circa 1900, 25½in. high.
$1,440 £640

Mahogany bracket clock
by John Taylor, Lon-
don, 46cm. high.
$1,465 £650

BRACKET CLOCKS

English Regency bracket clock in mahogany case, 20in. high. $1,465 £650

18th century bracket clock by Lancaster & Son. $1,630 £725

Late George III mahogany bracket clock by Lautier, 10¼in. high. $1,680 £745

Mid 18th century fruit-wood striking bracket clock, signed Thos. West, London. $1,700 £750

Late 19th century bracket clock by Ellis Depree and Tucker. $1,700 £750

Early 18th century grande sonnerie bracket clock signed John George Werndle Presburg, 1ft.6in. high. $1,700 £750

19th century bracket clock in mahogany case by Geo. Sharpe. $1,750 £780

Continental ebonised bracket clock by Joseph Keipmuller, 15in. high. $1,750 £780

Regency mahogany striking bracket clock by Panchaud & Cumming, London, 16in. high. $1,800 £800

Rosewood bracket clock by Jn. B. Cross, London, 19in. high. $1,970 £875

Mahogany bracket clock, signed Sam. Watson, London, 19in. high.
$2,025 £900

Thwaites and Reed bracket clock, in a rosewood case.
$2,140 £950

Victorian oak cased bracket clock by Joseph Penlington, Liverpool. $2,200 £975

Walnut striking bracket clock by Robt. Sadler, London, 14½in. high.
$2,370 £1,050

George III mahogany bracket clock by W. Wall, Richmond, 1ft.4½in. high.
$2,370 £1,050

Bracket clock by John Ward, 20in. high, circa 1790, in an ebonised case. $2,700 £1,200

Mid Georgian ebonised fruitwood striking bracket clock by Thos. Martin, London, 17in. high.
$2,700 £1,200

19th century mahogany bracket clock in Turkish style, 27¾in. tall.
$2,700 £1,200

BRACKET CLOCKS

George III mahogany bracket clock by Richard Webster, London, 18½in. high.
$2,700 £1,200

Small ebonised bracket clock by Rimbault, London, 1ft.5in. high.
$2,700 £1,200

George II lacquered striking bracket clock by Thos. Hunter, London.
$2,900 £1,300

Late George III striking bracket clock by Thos. Sutton, Maidstone, 15in. high. $2,900 £1,300

An early George III mahogany bracket clock by Ellicott, London, 1ft.4in. high. $3,000 £1,350

19th century bracket clock by Robert Simpson, London. $3,000 £1,350

Mid 18th century ebonised bracket clock by J. Thwaites, London.
$3,150 £1,400

English bracket clock by John Mitchell, circa 1725, in mahogany case, 19in. high. $3,150 £1,400

Ebony striking bracket clock by John Fort, London, 13¾in. high, circa 1700. $3,265 £1,450

Bracket clock by John Feylitz, London, 17in. high. $3,265 £1,450

Early George III bracket clock by John Dalgleish, Edinburgh. $3,265 £1,450

George III ebonised bracket clock by Edward Lister, 19in. high. $3,375 £1,500

George III satinwood clock by Smith & Son, London, 12½in. high. $3,600 £1,600

George III pearwood bracket clock, 23in. high, dial signed John Williams. $3,600 £1,600

A George I blue japanned quarter repeating bracket clock by Wm. Pain, London, 1ft.9in. high. $3,700 £1,650

George III musical bracket clock by Palmer of Holborn. $3,940 £1,750

19th century Japanese brass striking bracket clock, 165mm. high. $3,940 £1,750

George III mahogany bracket clock by George Peacock, 1ft.3in. high. $3,940 £1,750

BRACKET CLOCKS

Mahogany bracket clock, circa 1770, signed Richard Ward, Winchester, 18in. high. $3,940 £1,750

Late 18th century mahogany cased bracket clock by F. Zagnani, London, 24in. high. $3,940 £1,750

Tortoiseshell and repousse striking bracket clock by George Murgatroyd, London, 18in. high. $4,050 £1,800

George III mahogany bracket clock by John Robert & Silva, London, 2ft.2in. high. $4,275 £1,900

Late George III period mahogany cased domed top bracket clock, 16¾in. high, by Dwerrihouse Carter & Son, London. $4,500 £2,000

George III mahogany striking bracket clock by John Taylor, London, 19in. high. $4,500 £2,000

Red lacquered chiming bracket clock by McCabe, London, 22in. high.
$4,500 £2,000

George II quarter repeating bracket clock by Richard Peckover, London, 1ft.7in. high. $4,725 £2,100

Early 18th century bracket clock by H. Clarkson, Wolverhampton, in ebonised pearwood case, 19in. high. $4,725 £2,100

George III mahogany brac-
ket clock by James Mitchell,
London, 1ft.7in. high.
$4,725 £2,100

George III ebonised
bracket clock by John
Cowell, 2ft.2in. high.
$4,950 £2,200

Ebonised chiming bracket
clock by Francis Perigal,
London, 2ft.2in. high.
$4,950 £2,200

Japanned quarter repeating
bracket timepiece, 13½in.
high. $4,950 £2,200

George II bracket clock
in ebony case by John
Gordon, London, 17¾in.
high. $5,175 £2,300

Ebonised bracket clock
by Charles Gretton, circa
1700, 13½in. high.
$5,175 £2,300

Mahogany striking bracket
clock by John Wilcox,
19in. high. $5,175 £2,300

Late 18th century bracket
clock by Hare, London,
43cm. high.
$5,300 £2,350

George III ebonised bracket
clock by Robt. Henderson,
London, 1ft.7in. high.
$5,300 £2,350

BRACKET CLOCKS

Early 19th century mahogany musical bracket clock by J. & S. Farr, Bristol, 25in. high. $5,400 £2,400

Ebonised musical bracket clock by Markwick Markham, London, 1ft.9in. high. $5,400 £2,400

George III ebonised quarter striking bracket clock by J. Tregent, London, 17¼in. high. $5,850 £2,600

18th century eight-day walnut bracket clock by Lagisse et Fils, London. $6,075 £2,700

George III black japanned musical bracket clock by Wagstaffe, London, 1ft.9in. high. $6,300 £2,800

Late 18th century musical bracket clock by Robert Ward, London, 61cm. high. $6,500 £2,900

English bracket clock signed Vulliamy, London, 16in. high, in ebonised case. $6,750 £3,000

A Japanese striking bracket clock, 170mm. high. $6,750 £3,000

Ebony striking bracket clock by Henry Fish, London, 16¼in. high. $7,000 £3,100

16

18th century bracket clock by Richard Gregg, London. $7,300 £3,250

Dutch ebony gilt mounted bracket clock, 17in. high. $7,400 £3,300

Late 18th century mahogany quarter repeating bracket clock by William Dutton, 14in. high. $7,875 £3,500

Ebony veneered basket top, quarter repeating bracket clock by Sam. Marchant, London, 14in. high. $7,875 £3,500

George II walnut bracket clock by John Ellicott, London, 1ft.6in. high. $7,875 £3,500

A George III ebonised quarter repeating bracket clock by Thos. Mudge, 14½in. high. $7,875 £3,500

Early ebonised basket top quarter repeating bracket clock by William Cattell, circa 1685, 14½in. high. $9,000 £4,000

Small mahogany bracket clock by William Allam, London, 1ft.4in. high. $9,000 £4,000

Ebonised basket top bracket clock by John Barnett, London, 1ft.1in. high. $9,000 £4,000

17

BRACKET CLOCKS

Georgian musical bracket clock by R. Roskell, Liverpool, 34½in. tall.
$9,675 £4,300

Eight-day English fusee bracket clock in ebony case by A. Quiguer, London, circa 1687.
$10,500 £4,700

Early George III marquetry musical bracket clock, signed Eardley Norton, 2ft. 4½in. high.
$10,800 £4,800

George II walnut bracket clock by Samuel Whichcote of London.
$10,800 £4,800

Walnut bracket clock by Daniel Quare, London, 14in. high.
$11,250 £5,000

Elaborate bracket clock by William Vale, London, 36in. high, in padoukwood case.
$11,250 £5,000

George III rosewood chiming bracket clock, dial signed Vulliamy, London, 1ft.3in. high.
$12,150 £5,400

Bracket clock by Joseph Windmills, London, 14½in. high. $12,375 £5,500

17th century bracket clock by Daniel le Count, 13½in. tall. $12,375 £5,500

Ebony striking bracket clock by Chris. Gould, London, 15in. high. $12,950 £5,750

George III bracket clock by John Elliott. $13,500 £6,000

Rare olivewood basket top bracket timepiece by N. Hodges. $18,000 £8,000

Mid 17th century bracket clock in an ebony veneered case by Pieter Visbagh, 10in. high. $18,450 £8,200

Basket top quarter repeating bracket clock by D. Quare, circa 1695, 14in. high. $23,625 £10,500

Bracket clock by Joseph Knibb, London, 1685, in ebony case, 31cm. high. $25,875 £11,500

Ebony veneered bracket clock by Samuel Barkley and Thos. Colley, London, 1751-54, 35.5cm. high. $26,100 £11,600

Bracket clock by Joseph Windmills, circa 1695, in ebonised case. $27,000 £12,000

Bracket clock by Thos. Tompion, London, circa 1700, 40cm. high. $36,000 £16,000

CARRIAGE CLOCKS

Gilt spelter carriage clock, circa 1890, 6½in. high. $250 £110

Compass and thermometer clock with single train drum movement. $400 £180

Victorian silver carriage clock, with eight-day movement. $450 £200

Brass cased gong striking carriage clock, dial signed Pedler, 7½in. high. $520 £230

French clock with brass overlay on ebony, 1880, eight-day movement. $565 £250

Early 20th century champ leve enamel and gilt metal carriage timepiece, 8½in. high. $620 £275

Silver mounted carriage clock set with transparent ruby ground glass, maker's mark WW/WW, London, 1894. $655 £290

Gilt metal carriage clock by Shreve Crump & Low, Boston, 6in. high. $675 £300

Late 19th century gilt brass alarm carriage clock, probably by Brune, 7in. high. $855 £380

Liberty & Co. 'Cymric' silver and enamel clock, Birmingham 1904, 8cm. high. $900 £400

French miniature carriage clock, 3¼in. high, with silvered dial. $945 £420

Brass striking carriage clock with movement by Bolviller, Paris, 5½in. high. $990 £440

Gilt metal striking carriage clock by Paul Garnier, Paris, 5in. high. $1,080 £480

Gilt brass repeating alarm carriage clock, circa 1880, 7in. high. $1,250 £550

An alarm carriage clock by Hunt & Roskell, London, 6¼in. high. $1,350 £600

'One-piece' cased carriage alarm clock, 5¼in high. $1,350 £600

19th century repeater carriage clock, 1895, 6½in. high. $1,400 £625

19th century French gilt brass carriage clock by J. Soldarno. $1,465 £650

CARRIAGE CLOCKS

19th century petite son-
nerie carriage clock by
Joseph Berrolla, Paris.
$1,510 £670

French gilt metal carriage
clock, 8½in. high.
$1,520 £675

Repeat and alarm silver-
cased carriage clock.
$1,520 £675

Small polychrome enamel
mounted carriage time-
piece, 3¾in. high.
$1,520 £675

Brass gorge cased minia-
ture carriage clock, signed
J. J. L. Brevet, 3in. high.
$1,520 £675

Gilt metal striking carriage
clock by Drocourt, 6in.
high. $1,530 £680

French brass striking
carriage clock by Maurice
& Co., 6½in. high.
$1,575 £700

Small enamel mounted
carriage timepiece, 3½in.
high, in a red travelling
case. $1,645 £730

Rare brass four dial timepiece carriage clock, 6in.
high. $1,690 £750

Oval French brass striking carriage clock by Margaine, Paris, 5¾in. high.
$1,735 £770

Elaborate gilt metal striking carriage clock, 8¼in. high.
$1,735 £770

Carriage clock by Bolviller a Paris, 6½in. high.
$1,755 £780

Small oval carriage clock, 4¼in. high, in travelling case.
$1,800 £800

Small gilt metal quarter striking carriage clock by Chas. Frodsham, Paris, 4¼in. high.
$1,800 £800

A one-piece carriage clock in brass case, signed Paul Garnier Her de la Marine, Paris, 5½in. high.
$1,825 £810

Striking carriage clock inset with porcelain panels, 8¼in. high.
$1,860 £825

Quarter striking alarm carriage clock by C. H. Toutouze, Paris, 5½in. high.
$1,915 £850

French brass carriage clock in an Angalaise Riche case with porcelain side panels.
$1,915 £850

23

CARRIAGE CLOCKS

French repeater carriage clock in cloisonne enamel case. $1,915 £850

Enamel mounted alarm carriage clock, 5¾in. high. $1,950 £865

Oval alarm carriage clock signed Henry Capt. Geneve, 5¾in. high. $1,980 £880

Enamel mounted carriage clock in leather case, 6½in. high. $1,980 £880

A French timepiece carriage clock, 9½in. high. $1,980 £880

French brass porcelain mounted striking carriage clock, 5in. high. $1,980 £880

Gilt metal oval brass striking carriage clock by Drocourt, 5½in. high. $2,025 £900

Gilt metal porcelain mounted striking carriage clock, 7¾in. high. $2,025 £900

Gilt metal timepiece carriage clock by J. McCabe, London, circa 1840, 4½in. high. $2,025 £900

Gilt metal petite sonnerie striking carriage clock by Leroy, 4¼in. high.
$2,070 £920

English gilt metal carriage timepiece by Viner & Co., London, 4½in. high.
$2,080 £925

A French gilt metal porcelain mounted miniature carriage clock, 3¼in. high, by Drocourt.
$2,100 £935

19th century carriage clock in the Japanese manner, 6¾in. high. $2,125 £945

Early 19th century travelling clock by Gordon of London, 9in. high.
$2,200 £975

Repeat alarm carriage clock in a gorge case by Charles Frodsham & Co., Paris, circa 1875. $2,205 £980

Carriage clock in the Oriental manner, 6¾in. high.
$2,215 £985

Five minute repeating carriage clock by Henri Jacot, 7in. high.
$2,250 £1,000

Swiss silver gilt and enamel miniature carriage clock, 2¼in. high. $2,475 £1,100

CARRIAGE CLOCKS

Gilt metal grande sonnerie striking carriage clock by A. Margaine, 6¾in. high.
$2,475 £1,100

Grande sonnerie carriage clock by Glading & Co., Brighton, 7in. high.
$2,475 £1,100

19th century gilt brass and enamel mounted carriage clock, 6in. high.
$2,590 £1,150

French brass repeat alarm carriage clock by Leroy et Fils, 7¼in. high.
$2,590 £1,150

Silvered brass striking carriage clock by Drocourt, Paris, 5¾in. high.
$2,590 £1,150

Fine French gilt metal striking carriage clock, 6¾in. high.$2,590 £1,150

Silver gilt and enamel miniature carriage clock with mother-of-pearl dial, on green agate base, 2½in. high. $2,700 £1,200

Small quarter striking alarm carriage clock by Mortecot, Paris, 4¾in. high.
$2,700 £1,200

Grande sonnerie striking carriage clock by Drocourt, Paris.
$2,925 £1,300

A porcelain mounted alarm carriage clock, 5½in. high. $3,040 £1,350

Silver gilt and enamel miniature desk carriage clock with flared case decorated with scenes of the four seasons, 2¾in. square. $3,040 £1,350

Enamel mounted alarm carriage clock, case decorated with cloisonne scrollwork in red, blue and yellow. $3,150 £1,400

A polychrome enamel mounted alarm carriage clock by Leroy et Fils, Paris, 5¾in. high. $3,150 £1,400

Liberty & Co. 'Cymric' silver and enamel travelling clock, 1903, 15.2cm. high. $3,150 £1,400

Grande sonnerie alarm carriage clock signed Chas. Frodsham & Co., 5¾in. high. $3,375 £1,500

Porcelain mounted carriage clock, 6½in. high. $3,375 £1,500

Swiss silver gilt and enamel miniature carriage clock in the manner of Cartier, 2¼in. high. $3,600 £1,600

A carriage timepiece by Thwaites & Reed, London, 5¾in. high. $3,600 £1,600

CARRIAGE CLOCKS

Multi-piece carriage clock, London, 1841, 14cm. high, movement signed Parkinson & Frodsham. $3,825 £1,700

Brass and enamelled grande sonnerie striking carriage clock by Drocourt, 6in. high. $4,165 £1,850

English carriage clock by Edward Funnell, Brighton, 5in. high. $4,275 £1,900

A Biedermeier grande sonnerie alarm travelling clock, 9in. high. $4,275 £1,900

French brass cased grande sonnerie carriage clock, 7in. high. $4,500 £2,000

French brass calendar carriage clock in engraved case, 14cm. high. $4,950 £2,200

Late 19th century French brass carriage clock with grande sonnerie eight-day movement, 26cm. high. $4,950 £2,200

Large English repeating carriage clock signed T. E. Payne, Tunbridge Wells. $5,290 £2,350

An English quarter repeating carriage clock by E. & W. Smith, 8in. high. $5,625 £2,500

An enamel mounted grande sonnerie alarm carriage clock, 6½in. high. $5,965 £2,650

Grand petite sonnerie oval French carriage clock. $6,750 £3,000

An English repeater carriage clock by James McCabe, 6¾in. high. $8,325 £3,700

French grande sonnerie striking alarm calendar carriage clock by Drocourt, Paris. $8,550 £3,800

Early French gilt metal pendule de voyage, dial signed Dubois, Paris, circa 1780, 7½in. high. $9,000 £4,000

Small ebony veneered carriage clock by Vulliamy, London, circa 1840, 6½in. high. $14,650 £6,500

Grande sonnerie carriage clock by Charles Frodsham, London, circa 1917, 12cm. high. $38,250 £17,000

A grande sonnerie carriage clock by Nicole Nielson & Co., London, circa 1900, 15cm. high. $45,000 £20,000

Late 19th century carriage clock by Nicole Nielson & Co., in silver case, 11.5cm. high. $108,000 £48,000

Victorian china clock set with transfer decoration. $225 £100

Bronze figure on onyx clock set, 21½in. long, circa 1920. $450 £200

French eight-day striking mantel clock with matching pair of casolettes, 16in. high. $505 £225

Mid 19th century black marble, onyx and bronze clock garniture. $520 £230

Gilt spelter and marble clock garniture, circa 1900, clock 12½in. high. $520 £230

19th century French style clock garniture. $540 £240

Gilt bronze clock garniture, circa 1870, 16¾in. high. $540 £240

Late 19th century painted spelter and onyx clock garniture. $575 £255

Gilt bronze and marble clock garniture, circa 1880, clock 15¼in. high. $575 £255

Composed porcelain mounted gilt bronze clock garniture, circa 1880. $620 £275

Gilt bronze and white marble clock garniture, circa 1880, clock 27¾in. high. $675 £300

Late 19th century bronze and red and black marble clock garniture, clock 10½in. high. $675 £300

CLOCK SETS

French green marble and ormolu clock garniture, circa 1900. $745 £330

Gilt spelter clock garniture, circa 1880, clock 14in. high. $765 £340

Early 20th century ormolu mounted red tortoiseshell clock garniture, clock 15¾in. high. $765 £340

Early 20th century gilt bronze and Vernis Martin clock garniture. $790 £350

Early 20th century French gilt spelter and Paris porcelain clock garniture, clock 15½in. high. $790 £350

19th century French brass garniture de cheminee. $810 £360

Gilt bronze and porcelain clock garniture, circa 1890, clock 15¾in. high.$845 £375

Dark red marble and ormolu clock set, by L. Barbase, Paris.$900 £400

Gilt spelter 'Sevres' mounted clock garniture, 1880's, clock 16in. high.
$900 £400

Composed gilt spelter and porcelain clock garniture, circa 1880. $900 £400

Art Nouveau patinated metal clock garniture, circa 1900. $1,000 £440

French ormolu and cloisonne garniture of clock and candlesticks.$1,015 £450

CLOCK SETS

A patinated spelter composed clock garniture, stamped Le Message par J. Castellamaire, circa 1890, clock 19in. high. $1,015 £450

Late 19th century garniture of blue glass, clock by J. Leemans, Brussels.
                            $1,035 £460

Gilt spelter and porcelain mantel clock garniture, circa 1890. $1,125 £500

Gilt bronze and Sevres porcelain clock garniture, circa 1890, clock 16in. high.
                            $1,125 £500

A Berlin clock garniture, the white enamel dial enclosed in a rococo case, 25.5cm. high, 1849-70. $1,125 £500

Art Deco clock set of unusual design.
                            $1,180 £525

Gilt bronze and porcelain composed clock garniture, dial inscribed by Hry. Marc, Paris, circa 1890. $1,250 £550

Ormolu bronze and marble clock garniture by Briscard a Paris, 1870's, clock 18in. high. $1,300 £580

Gilt bronze and champleve clock garniture, circa 1890, clock 10¾in. high. $1,300 £580

Mid 19th century garniture de cheminee of Vienna porcelain. $1,350 £600

Gilt bronze and jewelled Sevres porcelain clock garniture, circa 1880. $1,350 £600

Brass and electrotype clock garniture, circa 1870. $1,350 £600

CLOCK SETS

Gilt bronze and champleve enamel clock
garniture, circa 1890, clock 12in. high.
$1,350 £600

Ormolu and marble clock garniture, circa
1900, dial signed Camerden and Foster,
New York, Made in France. $1,400 £620

Gilt bronze and Dresden porcelain clock
garniture, circa 1880, clock 14in. high.
$1,400 £620

Louis-Philippe ormolu and turquoise
porcelain clock set. $1,425 £625

Gilt bronze and jewelled Sevres composed clock garniture. $1,575 £700

French gilt metal and green onyx clock
set. $1,575 £700

36

Lacquered brass and polychrome enamel clock garniture with Arabic numerals, clock 18½in. high, circa 1900.
$1,700 £750

Gilt bronze clock garniture, clock in the form of an owl, circa 1890. $1,800 £800

Gilt bronze and Sevres clock garniture, circa 1880. $1,800 £800

19th century garniture de cheminee, 52cm. high. $1,825 £815

Cloisonne and ormolu clock set, circa 1870. $1,850 £825

Late 19th century ormolu and porcelain mounted clock set, 13in. high. $1,915 £850

37

CLOCK SETS

Gilt bronze and marble clock garniture, clock 26in. high, circa 1900.
$1,915 £850

Ormolu and porcelain composed clock garniture, 1880's, clock 16in. high.
$2,250 £1,000

Late 19th century cloisonne and onyx clock set. $2,475 £1,100

Dresden garniture de cheminee, clock 23in. high, candelabra 22in. high. $2,700 £1,200

Louis XVI style garniture of clock and two vases. $3,825 £1,700

Composed white marble and ormolu clock garniture, circa 1870, clock 24½in.,high.
$4,500 £2,000

38

Composed gilt bronze champleve enamel and painted opalescent glass clock garniture, circa 1880. $4,500 £2,000

Fine Christofle cloisonne enamel clock garniture, 1874, clock 16¼in. high.
$4,500 £2,000

rmolu and jewelled Sevres porcelain clock rniture, circa 1880, clock 20½in. high.
$6,750 £3,000

Barbedienne ormolu mounted red marble clock garniture, 1880's. $6,750 £3,000

Mid 19th century Sevres ormolu mounted rose-pompadour clock garniture.
$8,100 £3,600

Ormolu and bleu du roi Sevres porcelain garniture of mantel clock and a pair of matching candelabra. $15,750 £7,000

GRANDFATHER CLOCKS

Oak cased grandmother clock with a silver dial and Westminster chime.
$270 £120

English panelled oak longcase clock with engraved brass face in two sections.
$315 £140

Stylish modernistic clock, 1930's, 112cm. high.
$360 £160

Mid 19th century mahogany drum head longcase clock by J. Jeffrey.
$585 £260

19th century oak longcase clock by Robert Taylor, 72in. high.
$595 £265

Early 19th century thirty-hour oak cased grandfather clock. $745 £330

Wrought iron longcase clock, circa 1920, 65½in. high.
$745 £330

Oak cased grandfather clock, 80in. high, circa 1800.
$775 £345

Early 19th century oak cased grandfather clock with enamel dial.
$800 £355

Oak, mahogany and boxwood strung longcase clock by Barwise, London, 93in. high.
$810 £360

Edwardian longcase clock in chinoiserie case.
$845 £375

Early 19th century inlaid longcase clock by James Blaik, Peterhead.
$845 £375

Oak cased grandfather clock by Richard Alexander of Nursteed, circa 1780, 6ft.8in. tall.
$865 £385

An eight-day, oak cased clock by Bevan of Brecon.
$880 £390

Early 19th century oak longcase clock, 80½in. high. $900 £400

18th century Continental longcase clock with brass dial, 6ft. high. $955 £425

18th century mahogany longcase clock by Jn. Manby, Skipton, 89in. high.
$1,000 £440

Carved oak longcase clock by Goodchild of Bradford.
$1,000 £440

George II mahogany longcase clock, circa 1900, 64in. high.
$1,000 £440

Early 19th century mahogany longcase clock with painted face.
$1,060 £470

Oak grandfather clock by J. McKerrow.
$1,080 £480

Oak grandfather clock by Carmalt, Ringwood, 75in. high.$1,080 £480

Carved oak longcase clock by Samuel Whittaker.
$1,125 £500

Longcase clock in oak case, circa 1800.
$1,125 £500

Late 18th century longcase clock by George Mawman, Beverley.
$1,150 £510

'George IV' mahogany longcase clock, circa 1825, 97in. high. $1,120 £520

Small oak longcase clock by Washbourn of Gloucester, with 10in. dial, 6ft.6in. high. $1,205 £535

Mahogany longcase clock by Jn. & Wm. Mitchell, Glasgow, mid 19th century, 83in. high.
$1,285 £570

18th century mahogany longcase clock by Lawly, Abberford.
$1,350 £600

Early 19th century mahogany longcase clock, dial signed J. N. O. Green, Barnstaple, 82in. high. $1,350 £600

Mahogany longcase clock, circa 1830, 93in. high.
$1,350 £600

18th century eight-day clock in a carved oak case.
$1,350 £600

GRANDFATHER CLOCKS

Early Victorian mahogany longcase clock by John Monk, Bolton. $1,405 £625

An eight-day solid mahogany longcase clock by Wills of Truro, circa 1800. $1,440 £640

19th century mahogany cased longcase clock by Thos. Hawthorn, circa 1830. $1,485 £660

Mahogany longcase clock by Sam Collier, Eccles, 8ft.3½in. high. $1,520 £675

George III carved oak longcase clock, by Jon. Storr, York. $1,575 £700

18th century stained oak longcase clock, 88in. high. $1,575 £700

George III Scottish mahogany longcase clock, 6ft.3in. high. $1,610 £715

George III lacquer musical longcase clock by Pridham, London, 8ft.2in. high. $1,610 £715

18th century provincial red lacquer longcase clock by Edward Stevens, Boston, 80in. high.
$1,665 £740

Scottish longcase clock by David Greig, Perth, with shaped case.
$1,655 £740

Early 19th century mahogany longcase clock by Daniel Brown, Glasgow, 7ft.3in. high.
$1,690 £750

Oak longcase clock by V. Downs, Louth, with arched dial.
$1,690 £750

Late 19th century wickerwork longcase clock.
$1,735 £770

Late 18th century oak longcase clock by A. Dickie, Edinburgh. $1,780 £790

18th century longcase clock in black lacquered and painted case, by James Ferrey.
$1,800 £800

George III eight-day clock signed Nich. Le Maistre of Dublin, in mahogany case, 86in. high. $1,855 £825

45

GRANDFATHER CLOCKS

18th century eight-day longcase clock by Thomas Watts of Lavenham, 89in. high. $1,890 £840

George IV mahogany longcase regulation clock by Sherbourne, Aberdare. $1,915 £850

French provincial longcase clock with elaborate brass pendulum. $1,920 £875

Georgian oak longcase clock by J. Wainwright, Wellingborough, 6ft.7in. high. $1,980 £880

Oak longcase clock by E. Wickstead, Wolverhampton, circa 1750. $2,025 £900

Early 19th century carved oak longcase clock, 7ft.4in. high. $2,140 £950

Oak longcase clock by Samuel Whalley, Manchester. $2,140 £950

Edwardian mahogany longcase clock, signed by T. B. Cardwell, Liverpool. $2,140 £950

Eight-day long-case clock by Peter Boner, in marquetry case.
$2,195 £975

18th century long-case clock by Richard Wilson, London.
$2,195 £975

George II walnut clock, figured and crossbanded, by Thos. Moore of Ipswich.
$2,205 £980

18th century long-case clock by Walter Barr of Port Glasgow.
$2,230 £990

George III mahogany longcase clock by Thos. Hughes, London, 8ft.2in. high.
$2,250 £1,000

George III mahogany longcase clock by David Laing, Edinburgh, 7ft.2in. high.
$2,365 £1,050

George III longcase clock by Walter Turnbull, Caltown.
$2,365 £1,050

Inlaid oak longcase clock by Holroid of Wakefield.
$2,365 £1,050

47

Mid 18th century lacquerwork clock, by Zac Mountfort. $2,365 £1,050

Oak longcase clock by Corless Stockwell. $2,365 £1,050

Late 18th century carved oak longcase clock by J. Jones, Wrexham. $2,365 £1,050

Eight-day longcase clock in lacquer case, circa 1740, by Wm. Hall of Louth, 7ft.7in. high. $2,385 £1,060

George III eight-day longcase clock, signed Geo. Thatcher of Cranbrook, 90in. high. $2,430 £1,080

18th century lacquer longcase clock by Tillam Rudd. $2,430 £1,080

George II walnut provincial longcase clock, dial signed E. Greatrex, Birmingham, 7ft.3in. high. $2,590 £1,150

Georgian longcase clock by Henry Mayhew, Parham. $2,590 £1,150

Green lacquer long-case clock by E. Solomons of Canterbury, circa 1780.
$2,620 £1,165

Early 18th century lacquered longcase clock by J. Davis, London.
$2,700 £1,200

Mahogany longcase clock by Hugh Gordon, Aberdeen, 93in. high.
$2,700 £1,200

George III mahogany longcase clock, 84in. high, by J. Turnbull, Hawick.
$2,700 £1,200

Mid 18th century clock by E. Greatrex, Birmingham.
$2,700 £1,200

18th century inlaid mahogany longcase clock by Band & Hine.
$2,700 £1,200

Oak dead-beat longcase clock with brass dial, circa 1855, 92in. high.
$2,815 £1,250

George II walnut longcase clock, signed Tho. Peirte, London, 7ft.3in. high.
$2,815 £1,250

GRANDFATHER CLOCKS

Walnut longcase clock by Thos. Bolton, Manchester, 1791.
$2,845 £1,265

19th century, Jacobean revival oak longcase clock.
$2,845 £1,265

18th century mahogany longcase clock by Wyke & Green, Liverpool.
$2,845 £1,265

Oak longcase clock by H. White, Cheapside, with brass and silvered dial.
$2,925 £1,300

Late 18th century mahogany longcase clock by John Andrews of London, 87in. high.
$2,925 £1,300

George II yew and walnut longcase clock, 8ft.2in. high.
$2,970 £1,320

19th century oak cased grandfather clock with brass face.
$2,970 £1,320

Mid 18th century banded inlaid mahogany longcase clock by J. Ewer, London.
$2,970 £1,320

An early Georgian longcase clock, inscribed James Robinson, London, 7ft.7½in. high.
$2,920 £1,320

An oak longcase clock by John Kay, London, 7ft.4in. high.
$2,920 £1,320

Mahogany longcase clock by John Hamilton, Glasgow.
$3,015 £1,340

George II walnut longcase clock, signed Wm. Sayer, Devizes, 7ft.8in. high.$3,105 £1,380

George III inlaid mahogany longcase clock by W. Yeadon.
$3,150 £1,400

Oak longcase clock by Wm. Jackson, London.
$3,150 £1,400

George I walnut longcase clock by R. Peckover, London.
$3,150 £1,400

George II red japanned longcase clock by J. Lister, London, 8ft.2in. high.$3,150 £1,400

George III maho-
gany longcase clock,
7ft.10in. high, with
arched dial.
$3,220 £1,430

A mahogany long-
case clock signed
Hadwen of Liver-
pool, 1760, 9ft.
high.
$3,285 £1,460

Late 18th century
mahogany longcase
clock by Paul Cho-
tard of London, 7ft.
10in. high.
$3,330 £1,480

Early 18th century
walnut longcase
clock by G. Neale,
London, 8ft.9in.
high.
$3,375 £1,500

Late 18th century
longcase clock by
S. Langford, Lud-
low, in mahogany
case. $3,375 £1,500

Walnut longcase
clock by J. Fell,
London, 7ft.2in.
high.
$3,375 £1,500

Edwardian long-
case clock with
Whittington/ West-
minster chimes.
$3,500 £1,550

Arabesque marque-
try longcase clock,
signed Asselin,
London, 7ft. high.
$3,500 £1,550

Mahogany chiming longcase clock with brass dial, circa 1910, 93¾in. high.
$3,500 £1,550

Georgian mahogany longcase clock by Thos. Burton.
$3,500 £1,550

Ebonised clock by T. Newman, Dublin, circa 1700, 11in. dial.
$3,500 £1,550

George III mahogany longcase clock by S. Rimbault, 7ft. 11in. high.
$3,500 £1,550

  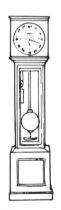 

Antique mahogany grandmother clock by J. Cunningham, Haddington, 62in. high. $3,500 £1,550

Louis XV style marquetry longcase clock, 7ft.7in. high.
$3,500 £1,550

Mahogany longcase regulator with jewelled pallets, 6ft.4in. high.
$3,600 £1,600

Georgian walnut longcase clock by T. Jenkinson, Sandwich.
$3,600 £1,600

GRANDFATHER CLOCKS

Small George III mahogany month regulator, 5ft.11in. high. $3,600 £1,600

Scottish George III mahogany longcase clock by J. Houden, Edinburgh, 6ft.10in. high. $3,600 £1,600

Early George III longcase clock by C. Smith, London. $3,715 £1,650

George III mahogany longcase clock by Wyke & Green, Liverpool, 7ft.6in. high. $3,715 £1,650

Small mahogany longcase clock of three months duration, height, without finial, 6ft.7in. $3,825 £1,700

Late 19th century mahogany regulator by T. Gamage & Sons, London, 107cm. high. $3,940 £1,750

Mahogany longcase clock by J. Barr, Houston, 80in. high. $3,940 £1,750

18th century Belgian longcase clock in oak. $3,960 £1,760

Sheraton style mahogany longcase clock by Wm. Stapleton, London, 7ft.1in. high. $3,960 £1,760

Mid Georgian mahogany longcase clock by N. Blondell, Guernsey, 9ft. high. $4,050 £1,800

Mahogany longcase clock by Barker of Wigan, 8ft.1in. high. $4,050 £1,800

18th century Flemish longcase clock by Joseph Glenet. $4,050 £1,800

Longcase clock by J. Wontner of Cornhill, London. $4,050 £1,800

18th century longcase clock by T. Wiggan, Bristol. $4,165 £1,850

Late 18th century Scottish regulator, signed T. Napier, Edinburgh, 82in. high. $4,210 £1,870

Georgian oak and mahogany longcase clock by N. Brown, Manchester, 7ft.2in. high. $4,275 £1,900

GRANDFATHER CLOCKS

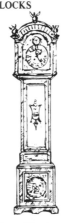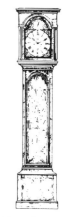

George III maho-
gany longcase clock
by Wm. Franklin,
London, 7ft.3in.
high.$4,275 £1,900

George III maho-
gany longcase clock
by Caleb Pitt, Frome,
86in. high.
$4,275 £1,900

Late George III
mahogany longcase
clock by Frodsham
& Son, Kensington,
8ft.4in. high.
$4,275 £1,900

Burr walnut long-
case clock by J.
Tipp, London, 7ft.
4in. high.
$4,295 £1,900

Walnut marquetry
longcase clock,
inscribed Barnes,
London.
$4,320 £1,920

A mahogany long-
case timepiece, dial
signed W. D. Fraser,
Elgin, 7ft.9in. high.
$4,320 £1,920

Small George III
mahogany regulator,
6ft.11in. high.
$4,320 £1,920

George III maho-
gany longcase
clock by H. Fisher,
Preston.
$4,330 £1,925

Edwardian long-
case clock, in
carved oak case,
8ft.2in. high.
$4,410 £1,960

Longcase clock, ven-
eered in walnut, dial
signed Wm. Mason,
London, circa 1760,
7ft.6in. high.
$4,455 £1,980

Inlaid mahogany
musical longcase
clock, front of
the movement sig-
ned M. Bradberry,
Leyburn, dated
1811.
$4,480 £1,990

Satinwood long-
case clock, signed
O. Vali, London,
80in. high, 1860-
80. $4,500 £2,000

Edwardian longcase
clock in carved maho-
gany case, 8ft.3in.
high. $4,500 £2,000

Georgian longcase
clock by D. Hubert,
London.
$4,555 £2,025

Fine lacquered
longcase clock,
circa 1740, 9ft.
high.
$4,725 £2,100

George III mahogany
longcase clock on
bracket feet, signed
Isaac Hurley, London,
7ft.8in. high.
$4,725 £2,100

57

GRANDFATHER CLOCKS

Walnut marquetry longcase clock by C. J. Crisp, Bristol, 7ft.4in. high.
$4,725 £2,100

18th century Flemish oak longcase clock, 7ft.9in. high.
$4,840 £2,150

Carved oak chiming longcase clock, circa 1890, 96in. high.
$5,000 £2,200

Ornately carved walnut longcase clock.
$5,000 £2,200

Figured mahogany longcase clock by J. Fenton, London.
$5,000 £2,200

Georgian mahogany longcase clock by Harrison, Liverpool.
$5,000 £2,225

Walnut longcase clock by John Ebsworth, circa 1690.
$5,175 £2,300

Walnut and marquetry longcase clock by Thos. Hall, London, 80in. high.
$4,725 £2,300

  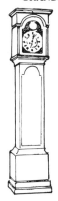 

18th century walnut and inlaid eight-day longcase clock by B. Fieldhouse.
$5,290 £2,350

Late 18th century bleached mahogany longcase clock by John Webb, 93in. high.
$5,290 £2,350

Early 18th century walnut longcase clock, engraved Tucker, London.
$5,515 £2,450

Large marquetry chiming clock, circa 1900, 105½in. high.
$5,625 £2,500

George III mahogany longcase clock by Holmes, London, 7ft.7in. high.
$5,625 £2,500

French month-going timepiece longcase regulator in mahogany case, 82in. high. $5,625 £2,500

George III mahogany grandmother clock, 5ft.3in. high, by J. Payne, Lenham.
$5,850 £2,600

18th century regulator by T. Church, Norwich.
$6,075 £2,700

GRANDFATHER CLOCKS

Longcase clock by R. Colston of London, circa 1700, 7ft. 3in. high.
$6,075 £2,700

George III mahogany eight-day striking clock by F. Perigal, 8ft.2in. high.
$6,075 £2,700

George III mahogany longcase clock by Vigne, London, 7ft.5in. high.
$6,190 £2,750

Mahogany regulator, dial signed Hone, Hammersmith, 6ft.9in. high.
$6,190 £2,750

Large carved longcase clock, 9ft.4in. high.
$6,190 £2,750

Small marquetry longcase clock by B. Wright, London, 6ft.6in. high.
$6,300 £2,800

Burr elmwood longcase clock by Wm. Sellers, London, 7ft. 1in. high.
$6,300 £2,800

Regency longcase clock with brass dial by N. Barwise, London.
$6,300 £2,800

George III mahogany longcase clock by Asa Hall Raynham, about 1800, 90in. high.
$6,525 £2,900

Marquetry and walnut longcase clock by M. Bunce, London, circa 1698. 7ft.6in. high.
$6,750 £3,000

Walnut marquetry longcase clock by A. Brown, Edinburgh, 7ft.6in. high.
$6,750 £3,000

Victorian mahogany longcase clock by Lees of Nottingham.
$6,750 £3,000

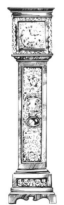

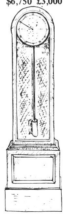

Edwardian inlaid mahogany longcase clock.
$6,750 £3,000

Late 17th century marquetry longcase clock by Ed. Norton, Warwick, 6ft.9in. high.
$6,750 £3,000

Mahogany longcase regulator, silvered dial signed E. H. Suggate, London, 6ft.2in. high.
$6,750 £3,000

Fine teak regulator, dial signed V. Kullberg, London, 5ft.10in. high.
$6,750 £3,000

GRANDFATHER CLOCKS

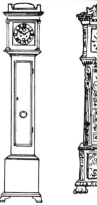   

Burr elmwood long-
case clock, signed
Markwick, London,
7ft.11in. high.
$6,750 £3,000

Ornately carved
walnut chiming
longcase clock.
$6,975 £3,100

Early 18th century
marquetry longcase
clock with eight-day
movement, by A.
Dunlop of London.
$6,975 £3,100

Early 19th century
longcase clock sig-
ned Robin aux
Galeries du Louvre,
6ft.10in. high.
$7,200 £3,200

  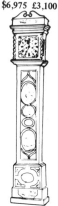 

Victorian mahogany
longcase regulator
with panelled plinth,
6ft.4½in. high.
$7,200 £3,200

18th century Dutch
walnut marquetry
longcase clock by
H. Borias, 91in.
high.$7,315 £3,250

Mid 17th century
striking longcase
clock by E. Card
of London, in
floral marquetry
case.$7,315 £3,250

Large mahogany
month going long-
case clock, late
1890's, 112in. high.
$7,425 £3,300

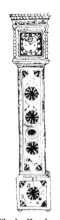

Edwardian longcase clock with three sets of chimes. $7,650 £3,400

Charles II walnut and parquetry longcase clock by Wm. Clement, London, 6ft.7in. high. $7,650 £3,400

George I burr walnut month longcase clock by D. Delander, 6ft. 11in. high. $7,875 £3,500

17th century longcase clock in walnut veneered case, with month movement signed J. Foster, 7ft. high. $8,100 £3,600

Boulle longcase clock in waisted arched case, mid 19th century, 81½in. high. $8,100 £3,600

A painted mahogany musical calendar longcase clock, 8ft. 10in. high. $8,100 £3,600

Mid 19th century French mahogany equation of time longcase clock, 6ft. 1in. high. $8,100 £3,600

Walnut marquetry longcase clock by F. Coulton in St. Anns, circa 1690, 8ft.5in. high. $8,100 £3,600

63

GRANDFATHER CLOCKS

18th century Dutch longcase clock by Gerrit Kolmer in walnut case, 96in. high.
$8,180 £3,635

Symphonium 'Sublime Harmony' musical longcase clock.
$8,325 £3,700

Marquetry longcase clock, dial signed by P. Garon, London, 8ft. high.
$8,550 £3,800

Early George III burr yew-wood longcase clock.
$8,550 £3,800

Marquetry longcase clock by T. Baker, Blandford, 6ft.6in. high, circa 1690.
$8,670 £3,850

George III regulator longcase clock by Brockbanks, London.
$9,000 £4,000

19th century French pedestal clock.
$9,000 £4,000

Marquetry longcase clock by J. Windmills, London, late 17th century, 7ft. 8½in. high.
$9,000 £4,000

A Dutch walnut longcase clock, 7ft. 11in. high.
$10,125 £4,500

Olivewood parquetry longcase clock, 6ft.10in. high, circa 1690.
$10,125 £4,500

Dutch marquetry longcase clock by Jacobus van der Hegge.
$10,125 £4,500

Late 17th century marquetry longcase clock by C. Gould, London.
$10,350 £4,500

18th century Dutch walnut musical longcase clock, 7ft.7in. high.$10,800 £4,800

A walnut quarter repeating longcase clock, 7ft.3in. high.
$11,250 £5,000

A George I walnut longcase clock by D. Delander, London, 7ft.9in. high.
$11,250 £5,000

Small longcase clock in a walnut marquetry case by J. Wise, circa 1680, 6ft.8in. high.
$11,250 £5,000

GRANDFATHER CLOCKS

Carved walnut eight-day longcase clock on eight bells and four gongs.
$11,250 £5,000

Early 19th century mahogany French longcase regulator timepiece.
$11,250 £5,000

Marquetry longcase clock by Thos. Farmer, circa 1685.
$11,700 £5,200

Early 18th century marquetry long-case clock by John Finch, London.
$11,700 £5,200

Late 17th century longcase clock by Andrew Brown, Edinburgh.
$11,700 £5,200

Burr maplewood month longcase clock, signed Fromanteel & Clarke, 8ft.8in. high.
$11,925 £5,300

Walnut and marquetry longcase clock by Wm. Garfoot, London, circa 1710.
$12,600 £5,600

Late 18th century Dutch marquetry longcase clock, signed Mc. W. Scholtz, Amsterdam.
$15,190 £5,750

   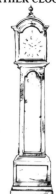

Late 17th century ebonised longcase clock signed E. Bir, London, 96in. high. $16,315 £7,250

Marquetry longcase clock by John Marshall, circa 1705. $16,875 £7,500

Early longcase clock by A. Fromanteel, London, 6ft.3in. high. $18,000 £8,000

18th century mahogany longcase clock by M. & T. Dutton. $19,350 £8,600

Small walnut longcase month clock by John Knibb, 6ft.6in. high. $22,500 £10,000

Late George II cream and apple green lacquered longcase clock, 2.53m. high, circa 1740, by I. Nickals. $22,500 £10,000

Longcase clock by G. Graham in burr walnut, 7ft.5in. high. $23,625 £10,500

Longcase clock by J. Knibb, circa 1685, in a fine marquetry case. $32,625 £14,500

67

Brass striking lantern clock, 10½in. high, 20th century.
$135   £60

19th century country-made lantern clock, 14in. high. $450   £200

Early 18th century brass cased lantern clock by I. Holmes. $1,015   £450

19th century brass cased lantern clock after R. Raiment, Bury, 23¼in. high.
$1,240   £550

English brass striking lantern clock signed Jno. Buffett, Colchester, 15in. high. $1,465   £650

Alarm lantern clock by Wm. Kipling, London, 1ft.3in. high. $1,620   £720

Lantern clock with 6½in. dial by T. Budgen, Reigate, 16in. high.
$1,800   £800

Early 18th century lantern clock in brass case, by Wm. Kipling, London, 36cm. high. $2,025   £900

Louis XV provincial wall timepiece, 14½in. high.
$2,025   £900

17th century brass lantern clock, by John Stakes, Dartford, 16in. high.
$2,250 £1,000

Small alarm wall timepiece, 5in. high.
$2,250 £1,000

Late 17th century brass lantern clock.
$2,365 £1,050

Lantern clock by Thos. Moor, 1ft.3in. high.
$2,365 £1,050

17th century brass lantern clock by Tho. Wheeler, 13in. high. $2,755 £1,225

Balance wheel lantern clock by Baker, complete with doors. $2,815 £1,250

Wing alarm lantern clock, 1ft.3in. high.
$3,040 £1,350

Miniature travelling verge lantern clock by Charles Groode, London.
$3,040 £1,350

Small lantern clock, signed Robert Dingley, London, 9in. high. $3,095 £1,375

LANTERN CLOCKS

Early 18th century brass lantern clock by John Draper, London, 14½in. high. $3,375 £1,500

Small brass lantern timepiece with alarm, circa 1700, 170mm. high. $3,600 £1,600

English brass striking lantern clock by Peter Closson, London, 11in. high. $3,715 £1,650

Lantern clock, circa 1690, by Joseph Windmills, London, 16in. high. $3,825 £1,700

Brass lantern clock by Stephen Levitt, circa 1690. $3,825 £1,700

Lantern clock dial signed Edward Stanton, London, 15in. high. $4,050 £1,800

17th century brass lantern clock with one hand. $4,275 £1,900

18th century Japanese lantern clock, 280mm. high. $4,275 £1,900

17th century brass lantern clock by John Read. $4,275 £1,900

Small lantern clock signed Sam Wichell, Piccadilly, 9in. high. $4,860 £2,160

Provincial lantern clock by E. Bilbie, circa 1675, 10in. high.
$6,075 £2,700

English brass quarter striking lantern clock, 16½in. high. $6,415 £2,850

English brass miniature lantern clock, unsigned, 9¾in. high.
$6,750 £3,000

English brass quarter striking lantern clock, 12¾in. high.
$6,750 £3,000

Small alarm lantern timepiece by Joseph Knibb, London, 7in. high, sold with a wooden bracket.
$6,750 £3,000

Lantern clock by Windmills, London, 1ft.4in. high, with an oak bracket. $7,315 £3,250

Lantern clock by John Knibb, Oxford, circa 1690, 17½in. high.
$12,150 £5,400

Large Carillon quarter striking lantern clock, 26in. high.
$14,065 £6,250

MANTEL CLOCKS

20th century walnut cased mantel clock. $25 £10

19th century American mantel clock in rosewood case. $55 £25

Victorian black marble mantel clock with brass fittings. $100 £45

China mantel clock, circa 1880, eight-day French movement. $125 £55

Edwardian inlaid striking mantel clock, circa 1900, 11in. high. $125 £55

Late 19th century walnut mantel clock with silverised and brass dial. $135 £60

French Edwardian inlaid mahogany mantel clock. $160 £70

American alarm clock, circa 1890. $160 £70

French mantel clock mounted in gilt metal cylinder movement. $190 £85

Inlaid balloon clock, circa
1890, French movement.
$215 £95

Victorian barometer, clock
and thermometer in oak
case, 13in. high.
$215 £95

Liberty & Co. 'Tudric'
pewter clock, after
1903, 17cm. high.
$250 £110

19th century clock with
striking movement in a
brass and ormolu case.
$250 £110

Victorian oak cased mantel
clock with drawer in the
base. $250 £110

Soft metal Art Nouveau
clock signed N. Bochin.
$270 £120

19th century French man-
el clock decorated in the
uhl manner. $270 £120

Late 19th century Ameri-
can cold painted cast iron
'Black Boy' timepiece, 1ft.
3½in. high. $270 £120

Massive marble clock, 1930's,
29.5cm. high. $295 £130

MANTEL CLOCKS

Victorian spelter mantel clock depicting an artist, 1ft.8in. high.$340 £150

Rosewood and parquetry mantel clock, circa 1880, 19¾in. high. $340 £150

Liberty & Co. 'Tudric' pewter and enamel clock after 1903, 18.75cm. high. $350 £155

Late 19th century brass cased mantel clock with enamel dial. $360 £160

Gilt metal and marble mantel clock, stamped Manning, Worcester, 19in. high, circa 1860. $360 £160

Gilt spelter and porcelain mantel timepiece, 1870's 15in. high. $370 £165

Pewter and enamel clock, circa 1905, 14.25cm. high. $370 £170

George III drum clock with brass inlay, circa 1820. $370 £170

20th century Italian painted mantel clock with bracket, 24½in. high. $400 £180

MANTEL CLOCKS

19th century French marble pillar clock.
$400 £180

German eight-day striking mantel clock, circa 1900.
$415 £185

Stained mahogany mantel clock, 15¾in. high, circa 1900. $415 £185

Liberty & Co. 'Tudric' pewter and enamel clock, circa 1905, 25.5cm. high.
$430 £190

Late 19th century gilt bronze and alabaster mantel clock, 15½in. high, dial signed Hry. Marc, Paris.
$430 £190

German movement Ting Tang clock in inlaid mahogany case.
$430 £190

Silver plated French clock depicting Louie Fuller, circa 1910. $430 £190

Art Deco bronze and marble clock, 26cm. wide, 1920's. $430 £190

An ornamental brass chiming clock with French Japy movement. $450 £200

75

Bronze mantel clock, dial with Roman numerals, circa 1860, 9½in. high. $450 £200

George III ebonised mantel clock by Paterson, Edinburgh. $450 £200

Late 19th century earthenware clock case by J. Vieillard, Bordeaux, 40.5cm. high. $450 £200

French ormolu mantel clock with white porcelain dial. $450 £200

Mid 19th century gilt bronze mantel clock, 11½in. high. $475 £210

Small Liberty & Co. pewter and enamel clock, 19.75cm. high, after 1903. $475 £210

An 'Hours Clock' by John Bell, 1851, in gilt on repousse copper. $500 £225

Black marble and bronze mantel clock, 23½in. high, circa 1870. $500 £225

Mahogany mantel timepiece, dial signed Barraud & Lund, London, 1798, 9½in. high. $520 £230

Black Forest trumpeter clock, circa 1860, 15in. high. $520 £230

Late 19th century mahogany mantel clock, dial signed Le Cheminant, 14¼in. high. $530 £235

French Empire clock in bronze and ormolu case. $530 £235

19th century marquetry cased mantel clock and stand. $560 £250

Art Deco mirror glass clock, 1930's, 33.75cm. long. $560 £250

Gilt brass and champleve enamel mantel clock, circa 1880, 13in. high. $285 £260

19th century inlaid mahogany mantel clock by Barnsdale. $285 £260

Art Nouveau wood clock, circa 1900, 35cm. high. $285 £260

French gilt metal clock of Louis XVI design, 11½in. high. $285 £260

MANTEL CLOCKS

Clock case in green marble surmounted by a bronze figure, circa 1900, 39cm. high. $600 £265

Early Martin Brothers clock case, 10½in. high, dated 10-74. $600 £265

19th century gilt metal Strutt desk clock, 127mm. overall height. $600 £270

19th century Dutch Delft clock with brass works, 18½in. high. $600 £270

Gilt bronze mantel clock, circa 1840, 16in. high. $620 £275

Mahogany mantel clock, circa 1900, 19in. high. $620 £275

Marble mantel clock, dial signed Charles Frodsham & Co., Paris, circa 1880, 14¾in. high. $630 £280

Patinated metal and glass clock, 38cm. high, 1930's. $630 £280

Silver and parcel gilt clock by Goldsmiths & Silversmiths Ltd., London, 1929, 13.5cm. high. $650 £290

78

Gilt spelter and porcelain mantel clock, circa 1890, 14¾in. high. $650 £290

Mid 19th century bronze and marble mantel clock, 21½in. high. $650 £290

Mid Victorian mantelpiece clock in brass and bronze mounted case. $650 £290

22in. tall gilt bronze clock, 19th century, in the form of an Indian building. $675 £300

Late 19th century Plaue on Havel clockcase, 40.5cm. high. $675 £300

Solid silver French carriage type clock, 1888, 4½in. high. $685 £305

Art Nouveau silvered metal clock case, circa 1900, 53cm. high. $700 £310

Small French mantel clock by Paul Garnier, Paris, 6in. high. $700 £310

Charles X ormolu mantel clock, 1ft. 3½in. high. $700 £310

MANTEL CLOCKS

Gilt bronze mantel clock, 1880's, 16in. high, with porcelain dial. $700 £310

French 19th century mantel clock. $710 £315

Gilt metal and marble mantel clock, circa 1880, 13in. high. $720 £320

A French world time clock with 24-hour dial, 13in. high. $720 £320

Clock from a gilt bronze clock garniture, dial with enamel Roman numerals, circa 1880. $720 £320

Late 19th century four glass and brass mantel clock, 11in. high. $720 £320

Gilt brass and champleve enamel clock, dial inscribed Coventry Lever Co., Birmingham, circa 1890, 12in. high. $720 £320

Small gilt metal mantel timepiece with enamel dial, 10in. high. $730 £325

Red boulle mantel clock, circa 1880, 16¾in. high. $745 £330

Lalique square clock case, 4¼in.
$755 £335

Gilt bronze and porcelain mantel clock, circa 1880, dial signed Dent a Paris, 11½in. high.
$765 £340

Gilt and patinated bronze and marble mantel clock, circa 1840, 23in. high.
$765 £340

Mid 19th century gilt bronze mantel clock, signed Leroy & Fils, Paris, 18½in. high.
$790 £350

Lalique frosted glass clock, 16cm. high, circa 1920.
$790 £350

Austrian F. Kunz musical mantel clock with two-air cylinder movement, circa 1880, 1ft.5in. high.
$790 £350

Gilt and silvered bronze mantel clock, circa 1870, movement signed Deniere a Paris, 18¼in. high. $790 £350

Regency mahogany mantel timepiece by Thos. Harlow, London, 15in. high. $790 £350

Early 19th century 'Louis XV' gilt bronze mantel clock, dial signed Priqueler A Lure, 16½in. high.
$790 £350

81

MANTEL CLOCKS

Mid 19th century boulle mantel clock, signed Fearn a Paris, 10½in. high. $790 £350

An alabaster rack timepiece with enamel dial, 1ft.5in. high. $800 £355

Late 19th century clock, with ormolu mounts, 16in. high. $820 £365

A French musical mantel clock, 1ft.9in. high. $820 £365

A desk clock in the form of a ship's wheel, circa 1850, 10in. high. $820 £365

Frederick Bull electric mantel clock in an arched rosewood case, 23cm. high, circa 1880. $820 £365

Louis XVI ormolu and white marble mantel clock, 16in. wide. $845 £375

Continental carved wood Art Nouveau clock case, circa 1900, 37.5cm. high. $855 £380

Bronzed brass mantel clock by Shuttleworth, Piccadilly, 16½in. high. $855 £380

82

Charles X gilt bronze mantel clock with outside count wheel, circa 1830, 14in. high. $900 £400

Gilt bronze mantel clock with outside count wheel, circa 1870, 25in. high.
$900 £400

Gilt bronze and enamel mantel clock, movement signed Howell James & Co., Paris, circa 1880, 11½in. high.
$900 £400

Doulton stoneware clock case, 8½in. high, circa 1880. $900 £400

Second Empire gilt and bronze mantel clock, circa 1860, 10in. high.
$925 £410

Gilt bronze and porcelain mounted mantel clock, circa 1870, 16in. high.
$925 £410

Late 19th century parcel gilt bronze lyre timepiece, with sunburst finial, 15½in. high. $945 £420

French mid 20th century painted enamel and gilt metal mantel clock in the form of a screen, signed CSK. $945 £420

Gilt and patinated bronze mantel clock, circa 1860, 18in. high, surmounted by a group of a Turk and his Horse. $945 £420

19th century clock with striking movement in an ormolu and boulle case. $960 £425

Early 20th century gilt metal and porcelain easel timepiece, 13¼in. high. $970 £430

Early 19th century brass and bronzed mantel clock, 15in. high. $970 £430

French gilt and patinated bronze mantel clock, circa 1850-75, 1ft.10in. high. $980 £435

Late 19th century gilt metal desk clock signed Robt. Roskell, London, 235mm. high.$980 £435

Gilt bronze mantel clock by Rocquet, Paris, 40cm. high. $1,015 £450

French Empire mantel clock in mahogany case, 50cm. high.$1,015 £450

Mahogany framed mantel clock with an unusual movement, 16½in. high. $1,015 £450

19th century English timepiece, dial inscribed Vulliamy. $1,015 £450

9ct. gold cased mantel clock on easel support, Goldsmiths & Silversmiths Co. Ltd., circa 1912, 11.6cm. high.
$1,035 £460

Regency period mahogany cased mantel clock, 13in. high.
$1,070 £475

Copper and satinised steel clock, 1930's, 31cm. high.
$1,080 £480

Bronze and ormolu mantel clock, 12in. high, circa 1860-80.
$1,080 £480

19th century white marble and ormolu mantel clock, 18in. high.
$1,080 £480

Red and black marble perpetual calendar mantel clock, circa 1860, 17½in. high.
$1,125 £500

Small mahogany mantel clock, dial signed Z. Reid, 9in. high.
$1,125 £500

White marble and gilt metal mantel timepiece by Vulliamy, London, 1ft.1½in. high.
$1,125 £500

A George III mahogany clock by Thos. Moss, London, 1ft.3in. high.
$1,125 £500

Mahogany mantel clock
by C. C. Webb, London,
9in. high. $1,160 £515

Ormolu and Sevres porcelain
mantel clock, dial signed
Raingo Fres., Paris, 12¾in.
wide, circa 1880.
$1,170 £520

Seth Thomas glass and
brass mantel clock with
enamel floral motif.
$1.170 £520

Late 18th century Meissen
oval frame, now converted
to a clock, 33.2cm. high.
$1,195 £530

Mid 18th century French
terracotta clock case,
24in. high. $1,215 £540

Early 19th century alarm
clock by Leblanc a
Boulogne, 11½in. high.
$1,240 £550

French Louis XVI style
boulle work mantel clock.
$1,240 £550

Mantel clock by Rollin,
Paris, in the form of a
large snail with a child
on its back.
$1,260 £560

Late 19th century four glass
and brass mantel clock, 14in.
high. $1,260 £560

Early 19th century French ormolu mantel clock, 1ft. 6in. high. $1,270 £565

Large gilt brass and painted glass mantel clock, circa 1880, 18¾in. high. $1,295 £575

Mid 19th century white onyx and ormolu mounted French striking clock. $1,295 £575

Large Liberty & Co. 'Tudric' pewter and enamel clock, after 1903, 32cm. high. $1,295 £575

Early 18th century gilt metal astronomical travelling clock by Wm. Winrowe, 10in. high. $1,350 £600

Gilt metal and pinchbeck striking mantel clock, 10½in. high. $1,350 £600

Directoire ormolu mounted white marble mantel clock, circa 1795, 15½in. high. $1,440 £640

A bronze and ormolu mantel clock with Sevres panel. $1,465 £650

Directoire ormolu mounted white marble timepiece, circa 1795, 13½in. high. $1,485 £660

MANTEL CLOCKS

Tortoiseshell and ormolu clock, circa 1870, 19in. high. $1,485 £660

Preiss clock with marble base, 1930's, 37cm. high. $1,485 £660

Early 19th century Directoire marble and ormolu mounted mantel clock, 22in. high. $1,510 £670

Porcelain and ormolu mantel clock, enamel dial with Roman numerals, 15in. high, circa 1880.
$1,530 £680

Gilt and patinated bronze mantel clock, dial signed Gille L'Aine, Paris, circa 1870, 21½in. high.
$1,530 £680

19th century French ormolu mantel clock. $1,530 £680

Late 18th century Louis XVI marble and ormolu mounted mantel clock, 21in. high. $1,600 £710

Liberty & Co. 'Tudric' pewter and enamel clock, circa 1903, 13.5cm. high.
$1,620 £720

Bronze and ormolu mantel clock, 12in. wide.
$1,620 £720

Louis XVI ormolu mounted white marble clock, 1ft.1in. high.$1,665 £740

Ormolu Strutt timepiece with eight-day movement, signed 'Made by Thos. Cole', 5½in. high. $1,680 £745

Ormolu French striking clock by Achille Brocot, circa 1850, 33cm. wide. $1,680 £745

19th century Dresden cased mantel clock, 11½in. wide. $1,690 £750

Restoration ormolu mantel clock, circa 1820, 1ft.7½in. high. $1,690 £750

Walnut mantel clock in well figured wood, circa 1850, 25¼in. high. $1,735 £770

Louis XVI ormolu mounted white marble mantel clock, 2ft. high, circa 1785. $1,735 £770

Empire ormolu and cut glass mantel clock, 19in. high. $1,755 £780

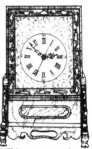

A Chinese rosewood table clock and stand, with enamel dial and gilt surround, circa 1800. $1,755 £780

19th century French ormolu and gros bleu porcelain mantel clock of Louis XVI design, 24in. wide. $1,800 £800

Louis XVI ormolu and white marble mantel clock, 1ft.2in. high. $1,800 £800

An ormolu malachite and lapis part clock garniture, circa 1860, stamped Bourdin, Paris. $1,800 £800

19th century boulle mantel clock with ormolu mounts. $1,800 £800

Late George III mahogany mantel clock by Hamley, London, 1ft.10½in. high. $1,800 £800

Large Meissen mantel clock, 23in. high, unmarked. $1,800 £800

Empire ormolu mantel clock, 22in. high. $1,845 £820

French mystery clock. $1,890 £840

German gilt metal striking table clock, 12.5cm. square. $1,890 £840

Louis XVI white marble and ormolu timepiece, enamel dial signed Schmit a Paris, 1ft.3in. high.
$1,970 £875

Mid 19th century Russian ormolu and malachite mantel clock, 12½in. high.
$1,970 £875

Louis XV ormolu clock, mid 18th century, signed James McCabe, London, 18in. high. $1,980 £880

Gilt bronze and Sevres mantel clock, dial signed Lepaute a Paris, circa 1880, 18½in. high. $1,980 £880

Large Goldscheider Art Nouveau terracotta clock, circa 1900, 95cm. high.
$2,050 £900

Viennese gilt metal mantel clock by Joseph Brasner, 7in. high. $2,050 £900

Ithaca parlour model calendar clock in walnut case, with double dial.
$2,050 £910

Early 19th century alarm clock, 11½in. high, Jura.
$2,070 £920

Ormolu and Sevres porcelain mantel clock on gilt wood stand, circa 1880, 19¾in. high. $2,070 £920

MANTEL CLOCKS

Liberty & Co. silver and enamel clock, 6in. high.
$2,140 £950

19th century boulle and gilt bronze clock, by Martinot a Paris, 32in. high.
$2,140 £950

Early 19th century Directoire marble and ormolu mounted mantel clock, 30in. high. $2,250 £1,000

19th century French gilt and cast brass lyre clock.
$2,250 £1,000

Lalique glass 'siren' clock, circa 1925, 27.5cm. high.
$2,250 £1,000

Small Louis XVI white marble and ormolu mantel clock, dial signed Leroy a Paris, 1ft.2½in. high. $2,250 £1,000

Vienna gilt metal mounted clock case. $2,475 £1,100

Gilt bronze and porcelain mantel clock, circa 1880, 20in. high. $2,475 £1,100

19th century French mantel clock, 28in. high.
$2,475 £1,100

Black Forest organ clock, in Gothic styled oak case, 34½in. high.
$2,700 £1,200

Preiss bronze and ivory figure of a kneeling dancer supporting a clock.
$2,700 £1,200

Mahogany cased clock with tulipwood banding, 25in. high.
$2,700 £1,200

19th century ormolu and porcelain mantel clock by Potonie of Paris, 22½in. tall.
$2,700 £1,200

A two-faced mahogany ship's clock by Litherland Davies & Co., Liverpool, circa 1840.
$2,815 £1,250

19th century French lyre shaped mantel clock.
$2,815 £1,250

Mid 19th century malachite mounted ormolu and silvered metal mantel clock, 7½in. high.
$2,925 £1,300

Viennese gilt wood David and Goliath grande sonnerie mantel clock, 19in. high.
$2,925 £1,300

Regency ormolu mounted tortoiseshell veneered religieuse, 23in. high.
$2,925 £1,300

Brass timepiece in a floral engraved case by James Muirhead & Son.
$3,040 £1,350

20th century rococo boulle mantel clock with enamel dial, 40½in. high.
$3,040 £1,350

Late 19th century ormolu and bronze mantel clock with urn surmount.
$3,150 £1,400

Early 19th century mahogany grande sonnerie mantel clock by Dubois & Fils, Jura, 10in. high.
$3,150 £1,400

A Louis XIV boulle mantel clock signed Thuret a Paris, 3ft.2in. high. $3,375 £1,500

Brass inlaid ebonised travelling mantel clock, 8in. high.
$3,375 £1,500

Chrome and glass clock, 20th century, by Adnet.
$3,375 £1,500

An ormolu and verde antico marble mantel clock, 2ft.3in. high.
$3,375 £1,500

German hexagonal table clock with movement, signed Michael Fabian Thorn, 11cm. diam.
$3,500 £1,550

Restoration bronze and ormolu watch stand, 5¾in. high, circa 1820. $3,600 £1,600

Mid 19th century table clock by Thomas Cole, 6in. high. $3,600 £1,600

Louis XIV rosewood and inlaid religieuse, signed Le Mayre a Paris, 1ft.8½in. high. $3,600 £1,600

Early 19th century French ormolu mantel clock, 16in. high. $3,600 £1,600

Viennese enamelled copper clock, 39cm. high, circa 1910. $3,715 £1,650

Dutch gilt travelling clock by Johannes van Ceulen. $3,940 £1,750

Early French gilt metal pendule de voyage, by Beckera, 8½in. high. $3,940 £1,750

Lalique clock, 14¾in. high. $3,940 £1,750

Ebonised and ormolu mounted mantel clock by Johnson, London, circa 1800. $3,940 £1,750

95

French ormolu and porcelain mounted portico clock, 20½in. high. $3,940 £1,750

French Empire 'vase' clock with metal urn, 17in. high. $4,050 £1,800

19th century white marble calendar mantel clock, 1ft. 4in. high. $4,275 £1,900

George III mahogany balloon mantel clock by Ellicott, London, circa 1790, 19½in. high. $4,275 £1,900

A Meissen armorial rococo clock case and stand, 54.5cm. high, circa 1735. $4,275 £1,900

Late 18th century Louis XVI ormolu and patinated bronze mantel clock, 17½in. high. $4,500 £2,000

Rosewood cased eight-day mantel chronometer by John Arnold. $4,725 £2,100

Patinated and gilt bronze terrestrial globe clock, stamped G. H. Bte. SGDS, circa 1901, 26½in. high. $4,950 £2,200

Good five-sided gilt metal table timepiece, 6¾in. high. $5,400 £2,400

MANTEL CLOCKS

Urn shaped revolving band ormolu clock by Paul Rimbault. $5,625 £2,500

Large Louis XV gilt bronze mantel clock, dial signed Monbro Aine a Paris, circa 1840, 35½in. high.
$5,625 £2,500

Early Louis XVI ormolu mantel clock signed Gilles L'Aine, 22¾in. high.
$5,850 £2,600

Inlaid mantel clock designed by Josef Olbrich, 1902, 35cm. high. $5,850 £2,600

Late 18th century Flemish painted mantel clock, 2ft. 4in. high. $5,850 £2,600

19th century French brass striking calendar clock, 18in. high. $5,850 £2,600

Late 18th century ormolu mounted French clock by Roquelon, Paris, 4ft.6in. high. $6,075 £2,700

19th century lyre clock in porcelain case, movement by Kinable. $6,300 £2,800

18th century clock by John Saunders, with a musical movement. $6,750 £3,000

97

MANTEL CLOCKS

George III tortoiseshell musical clock for the Turkish market, by Geo. Prior, London, 31in. high.
$6,750 £3,000

17th century hexagonal table clock by Plattlico Erhardo, 130mm. diam.
$6,750 £3,000

French ormolu mantel clock by Ferdinand Berthoud a Paris, 2ft.8in. high.
$7,650 £3,400

Gilt and patinated bronze globe timepiece, circa 1880, 29¾in. high, movement stamped Chles.
$7,875 £3,500

German tabernacle clock, 9in. high. $8,665 £3,850

18th century ormolu mounted bracket clock, 3ft.5½in. high. $9,000 £4,000

Rosewood mantel clock by Arnold Frodsham, London, 11in. high. $9,450 £4,200

Silver desk clock by Faberge with circular enamel dial, 4¼in. diam.
$9,900 £4,400

Shelf clock by Aaron Willard in inlaid mahogany case, circa 1820. $10,575 £4,700

Louis XVI ormolu clock,
20½in. high.
$11,250 £5,000

Lalique glass clock 'Le jour
et la nuit', 38.75cm. wide,
1920's. $11,250 £5,000

17th century German table
clock, 350mm. high.
$11,590 £5,150

Striking mantel clock by
Breguet in mahogany
case, 285mm. high.
$12,150 £5,400

A lion mantel clock, ena-
mel dial signed Lepaute a
Paris, 1ft.10½in. high.
$12,150 £5,400

Striking table clock by
Jeremias Pfaff, circa 1700,
150mm. high.
$12,150 £5,400

19th century Sevres and
ormolu clock, 32in. high
by 28in. long.
$13,000 £5,750

Rare boulle, ormolu moun-
ted, musical calendar clock
by John Ellicott.
$13,000 £5,750

Early 17th century gilt
metal automaton lion
clock, 350mm. high.
$14,850 £6,600

MANTEL CLOCKS

Louis XV ormolu and Meissen porcelain monkey clock, circa 1740, 13¾in. high.
$15,750 £7,000

German gilt metal table clock by Jacob Wideman, 14.5cm. square, circa 1650.
$17,550 £7,800

A 19th century Japanese striking screen clock, by Takamura Takesuke, 270mm. high.
$17,550 £7,800

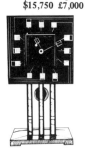

Domino clock by Charles Rennie Mackintosh, circa 1917, 10in. high.
$18,000 £8,000

Rare calendar mantel clock, 2ft. high.
$22,500 £10,000

A Louis XVI ormolu mantel clock, signed Bouchet du Roy a Paris, 22in. high.
$27,000 £12,000

A verge travelling clock by Johannes Van Cuelen.
$27,000 £12,000

Early 19th century ormolu mounted Blue John clock by A. R. Simons of Paris.
$27,000 £12,000

English 17th century table clock by Robert Grinkin, London, case 4½in. square.
$36,225 £16,100

Alarm day and night clock by John Hilderson.
$40,500 £18,000

Automaton clock, Augsburg, 1627. $41,500 £18,500

Lavender jade and black onyx desk clock.
$45,000 £20,000

17th century Flemish musical clock, signed Jean Knaeps, Liege, 2ft.11in. high. $50,000 £22,500

Candle alarm table clock by Pierre Fromery, Berlin, circa 1690, 26cm. high. $54,000 £24,000

16th century gilt metal Strasbourg quarter striking astronomical clock.
$86,500 £38,500

Louis XV musical clock in ormolu, bronze and Vernis Martin, 29in. high.
$130,000 £57,500

Rare precision clock by Thomas Mudge, in green shagreen case.
$170,000 £75,000

Augsburg tabernacle clock of 1700, veneered with tortoiseshell and stained horn.
$180,000 £80,000

101

SKELETON CLOCKS

Brass skeleton clock with enamel dial, circa 1890, 15¼in. high. $450 £200

An original Victorian skeleton timepiece, circa 1860. $730 £325

Skeleton timepiece with brass chapter ring, 10¾in. high.$950 £425

Skeleton clock by Hatfield & Hall, Manchester, 12½in. high. $1,400 £625

Skeleton timepiece by Barrauds, London, 1ft. 3in. high. $1,690 £750

Skeleton clock by Smith & Sons, Clerkenwell, 1ft. 4½in. high.$2,250 £1,000

Unusual timepiece skeleton clock, 20in. high, with glass dome. $2,700 £1,200

Large English striking skeleton clock, 22in. high. $2,925 £1,300

An early 19th century skeleton clock of 'rafter' construction. $3,265 £1,450

Rare chiming calendar skeleton clock, 1ft.7in. high.
$4,050 £1,800

A long duration Dutch skeleton clock, 2ft.5in. high. $4,500 £2,000

English brass chiming skeleton clock, 20in. high.
$5,400 £2,400

Brass cathedral skeleton clock signed C. Fiedemann, Liverpool.
$5,625 £2,500

Rare epicyclic skeleton clock, 10in. high, with a glass dome.
$6,300 £2,800

Fine skeleton clock by James Condliff, Liverpool, 20½in. high, with glass dome.
$8,550 £3,800

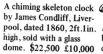
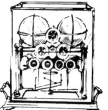

Early skeleton clock by Hubert Sarton, 1ft.5½in. high. $8,550 £3,800

A chiming skeleton clock by James Condliff, Liverpool, dated 1860, 2ft.1in. high, sold with a glass dome. $22,500 £10,000

Astronomical skeleton clock, by James Gorham, 19th century. $45,000 £20,000

103

WALL CLOCKS

Early 20th century oak cased wall clock. $90 £40

Late 19th century mahogany framed wall clock with enamel dial. $115 £50

19th century American mahogany framed Seth Thomas wall clock. $135 £60

19th century cased wall clock with octagonal head. $170 £75

Victorian Vienna style enamel dialled wall clock with Tunbridgeware style inlay. $180 £80

Vienna spring regulator clock, in oak case, circa 1880, 24in. high. $215 £95

American wall clock with white enamel dial, in walnut case, 74cm. high. $225 £100

Gilt metal wall clock, circa 1850, 20¾in. high. $225 £100

Inlaid American eight-day clock, circa 1890, 2ft.4in. high. $225 £100

Victorian papier mache wall clock by E. Fixary.
$315 £140

Bundy time recorder in oak case, 1.38m. high.
$315 £140

19th century mahogany wall clock with enamel dial by Johnson, York. $385 £170

Elaborate Victorian mahogany framed wall clock with brass pendulum.
$400 £180

19th century French eight-day striking clock, circa 1880, 31in. high.
$450 £200

19th century oak cased wall clock with ormolu decoration. $450 £200

19th century French wall clock with porcelain face and painted surround.
$495 £220

Walnut Vienna regulator, circa 1900, 42in. high, with enamel dial.
$495 £220

Antique rosewood cased wall clock, circa 1840, 23in. high.
$505 £225

WALL CLOCKS

Mid 19th century mahogany wall timepiece, dial signed Robt. Mack, Clerkenwell, 16in. high. $565 £250

19th century cuckoo clock in walnut case, 30in. high. $565 £250

Tavern wall clock in oak case, circa 1850, 56in. high. $540 £240

Stained oak wall clock, Austrian, circa 1880, 38in. high. $720 £320

18th century hooded wall clock in ebonised case, inscribed Ratcliff W. Pool. $790 £350

Mid 19th century Viennese regulator clock with ebonised case, 48in. high. $810 £360

Walnut cased Vienna regulator signed 'W. Schonberger, Vienna', 49in. high. $900 £400

Late 19th century French musical picture clock, 39in. wide. $900 £400

Gilt bronze cartel clock with outside count wheel, 17in. high, circa 1870. $945 £420

Custom mahogany weight driven banjo timepiece, dial signed Elmer O. Stennes, Mass. $945 £420

An unusual musical picture clock depicting the Houses of Parliament, circa 1870. $945 £420

Late 19th century Vienna regulator clock. $970 £430

Act of Parliament wall clock with black japanned trunk door. $970 £430

A Sevres gilt metal mounted pendant clock, 46cm. high, circa 1880. $1,080 £480

London silvered dial mahogany verge wall clock by Thornton, circa 1790. $1,125 £500

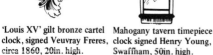

'Louis XV' gilt bronze cartel clock, signed Veuvray Freres, circa 1860, 20in. high. $1,125 £500

Mahogany tavern timepiece clock signed Henry Young, Swaffham, 50in. high. $1,300 £575

Louis XVI ormolu cartel timepiece, circa 1780, 16½in. high. $1,350 £600

WALL CLOCKS

Small mahogany quarter striking wall clock, 9½in. diam. $1,460 £650

Gilt metal wall clock by Chas. Nicolas de Hemant, Paris, circa 1760. $1,400 £625

Late 18th/early 19th century French gilt metal repeating wall clock by Perache, Paris, 22in. high. $1,485 £660

18th century French wall clock, 10½in. high. $1,520 £675

Early 20th century battery driven electric wall timepiece by the Brillie Bros., 18in. high. $1,690 £750

A mahogany wall timepiece by James McCabe, London, 8½in. high. $1,690 £750

Dutch Staartklok with carved wall bracket, 4ft.5in. high. $1,800 £800

Black and gold lacquered tavern timepiece clock, 54in. high. $1,800 £800

'Louis XVI' gilt bronze cartel clock, dial signed Paris, circa 1870, 33in. high. $1,845 £820

George III master clock
by Ablitt, Ipswich, 1.68m.
$2,140 £950

18th century South German
Telleruhr, 1ft.5½in. high.
$2,250 £1,000

Japanese weight driven wall
timepiece, 16in. high.
$2,250 £1,000

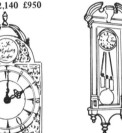

18th century wall clock
signed W. & J. Kipling,
London, 1ft.2in. high.
$2,250 £1,000

Three weight Vienna regu-
lator, circa 1880.
$2,250 £1,000

18th century Friesland
Stoelklok, 2ft.3in. high.
$2,475 £1,100

German Telleruhr with con-
centric calendar ring, 20½in.
high. $2,475 £1,100

Dutch Staartklok, 50in.
high. $2,590 £1,150

German Zappler clock, lack-
ing pendulum, 11½in. high.
$2,590 £1,150

109

Act of Parliament clock in chinoiserie case.
$2,590 £1,150

Bristol example of an Act of Parliament clock by Wm. Preist. $2,700 £1,200

Oak observatory wall regulator by T. Cooke & Sons, 4ft.7in. high.
$2,925 £1,300

Act of Parliament clock in a black lacquer case.
$3,375 £1,500

Dutch Friesland clock with painted dial, 27in. high.
$3,375 £1,500

A small wall clock signed George Prior, London, 5in. high. $3,825 £1,700

18th century Friesland wall clock with verge movement. $3,825 £1,700

18th century Friesland Staartklok. $4,950 £2,200

French gilt wood cartel clock, signed J. Marti et Cie, 39in. high. $5,175 £2,300

Mahogany wall regulator dial signed Dent, London, 4ft.4in. high.
$5,175 £2,300

Early Louis XVI ormolu cartel timepiece, 1ft.9in. high, circa 1775. $5,700 £2,500

Early striking clock by James Cowpe, London, circa 1665, 17in. high.
$6,300 £2,800

Walnut striking hooded wall bracket clock by John Ellicot. $6,975 £3,100

Austrian fruitwood wall regulator, 4ft.10in. high.
$6,975 £3,100

Act of Parliament timepiece by Jn. Wright of Dorking.
$7,200 £3,200

A 17th century Italian night clock in ebony case, 36½ x 22in. $7,300 £3,250

Dutch walnut hanging wall bracket clock, 31in. high.
$7,300 £3,250

Early 19th century Viennese walnut grande sonnerie wall clock, 42in. high.
$9,000 £4,000

WATCHES

Silver pair cased pocket watch by Joe Downs of London, with enamelled dial. $170 £75

Silver plated Swiss watch by J. G. Vickery, London, with bulb to light face, 4½in. high. $225 £100

Gold hunting cased keyless lever watch by Hasluck Bros., London, 1893, 48mm. diam., with gold chain and fob.
$450 £200

Watch in silver case by Lister of Halifax, dated 1774. $520 £230

19th century gold detached lever watch by Morris Tobias, 50mm. diameter.
$610 £270

Gold lever watch by F. B. Adams of London, 1835, 43mm. diam. $645 £285

Silver pair cased verge watch by Worke of London, mid 18th century, 51mm. diam.
$700 £310

Gold watch by Courvoisier et Cie, 1820, in oval silver case. $700 £310

Gold verge watch by Moon & Son, London, hallmarked 1812, 46mm. diam.$700 £310

Pedometer watch signed by Spencer & Perkins, London, 52mm. diam., circa 1780. $755 £336

Gold open faced lever watch by James McCabe, London, 1916, 41mm. diam., with gilt metal chain.$765 £340

Slim gold keyless lever dress watch, 42mm. diam., by Audemars Piguet & Co., $790 £350

Gold cylinder watch by James Tregent, London, circa 1800, 54mm. diam. $790 £350

Swiss gold and enamel cylinder watch by F. L. Achinard & Nouveau, Geneva, 33mm. diam. $900 £400

Silver pair cased verge watch, signed Thos. Gorsuch, Salop, 56mm. diam. $900 £400

Mahogany cased sedan watch by Edward Bradley, London, 85mm. diam. $970 £430

Fine 9ct. gold self-winding wrist watch by Harwood, with luminous numerals and hands, 1924, 29mm. diam. $1,015 £450

Gold and enamel cylinder watch by Bautte & Co., Paris, 19th century, 36mm. diam. $1,035 £460

Silver pair cased rack lever watch by Morris Tobias, London, hallmarked 1813, 57mm. diam. $1,070 £475

Cartier gold breast pocket clip watch, 1930's, 5.3cm. $1,070 £475

Gold cylinder watch by Rentzch of London, hallmarked 1826, 45mm. diam. $1,160 £515

Gold and turquoise set cylinder watch by Grant, London, 1819, 44mm. diam. $1,200 £530

Gold half hunting cased Montre a Tact by Bourdin a Paris, 43mm. diam. $1,215 £540

Early 19th century silver verge watch by Vaucher of Paris, 53mm. diam. $1,215 £540

A gold duplex watch by James McCabe, London, 1829, 50mm. diam. $1,240 £550

Gold and enamel cylinder watch by Muller, Geneva, 33mm. diam. $1,240 £550

Gold cylinder watch by L'Epine, early 19th century. $1,260 £560

Silver pair cased false pendulum verge watch by Marke Hawkins, 53mm. diam.   **$1,300 £580**

Silver pair cased verge watch signed Corn. Herbert, London, 58mm. diam.
   $1,350 £600

Verge watch by Burdet of London, about 1740, with silver pair cases.
   $1,350 £600

Swiss silver keyless mystery watch signed A. S. & P. Mysterieuse, Brevete S. G. D. G., 53mm. diam.
   $1,440 £640

Gold open faced quarter repeating keyless lever chronograph, dial signed F. A. Chandler, 51mm. diam.   **$1,465 £650**

French gold cylinder watch by Thouret, Paris, 33mm. diam.   **$1,530 £680**

Gold and enamel verge watch by Hessen, Paris, 18th century, 48mm. diam.   **$1,575 £700**

Gold hunter pocket watch with inner case and dome, set with five portrait miniatures.   **$1,575 £700**

Gold pair cased rack lever watch by Robert Roskell, Liverpool, 55mm. diam.
   $1,600 £715

Quarter repeating cylinder watch by F. Desvarieux of Rouen, 46mm. diam. $1,690 £750

Early 19th century pair cased key wound verge watch by Charles Cabrier, London. $1,755 £780

Silver quarter repeating alarm verge watch, signed Paul Beauvais, London, 55mm. diam. $1,755 £780

Silver pair cased verge watch by Markwick, London, circa 1710. $1,755 £780

Gold savage two-pin lever watch by G. Cashard, London, 1827, with heavy gold chain and fob seal. $1,800 £800

Gold pair cased rack lever watch, by P. Leyland & Co., Liverpool, 54mm. diam. $1,800 £800

Gold lever watch by D. Glasgow, London, 50mm. diam. $1,800 £800

Gold hunting keyless lever chronograph by Samuel Dixon, 50.5mm. diam. $1,800 £800

Silver gilt pair cased centre seconds cylinder watch by Justin Vulliamy, 58mm. diam. $1,860 £825

Fine gold keyless lever watch by Charles Frodsham, London, 1884, 50mm. diam.
$1,935 £860

Silver cased pocket watch, signed Thos. Earnshaw.
$1,980 £880

Gold open faced split seconds keyless·chronograph by Tiffany & Co. $2,025 £900

19th century gold quarter repeating independent centre seconds lever watch by Lepine, Paris, 47mm. diam. $2,025 £900

Gold hunting cased lever watch by R. H. Goddard, London, 1900, 53mm. diam. $2,025 £900

Repousse gold pair cased watch by Ellicott, London, 1733, 49mm. diam.
$2,200 £975

Multi-colour gold verge watch by Horne & Ashe, London, 1809, 47mm. diam. $2,200 £980

Silver cased watch by Abraham Louis Breguet, circa 1805.$2,250 £1,000

Small gold and turquoise set verge watch by Moulinie Bautte & Moynier, Geneva, circa 1830, 27mm. diam.
$2,365 £1,050

117

Italian gilt metal verge watch by Marc Blondel, Naples, 62mm. diam.
$2,365 £1,050

Gold cased verge watch by Benjamin Webb, London, 1802, 61mm. diam.
$2,475 £1,100

Silver pair cased watch, circa 1720, by George Graham. $2,475 £1,100

Gold open faced fuseee keyless watch by Barraud & Lunds, 1902, 52mm. diam. $2,590 £1,150

Quarter repeating cylinder watch by Leroy et Fils, Paris, circa 1820, 51mm. diam. $2,700 £1,200

Large silver pair cased verge watch, signed Wm. Smith, 81mm. diam.
$2,815 £1,250

Swiss calendar repeating watch by Perrenoud in a carved gold case.
$3,040 £1,350

Clock watch in tortoise-shell outer case by Justin Williami, circa 1670.
$3,040 £1,350

Gold quarter repeating cylinder watch by D. F. Dubois, Paris, circa 1790, 42mm. diam.
$3,040 £1,350

Gold quarter repeating cylinder watch, by Ellicott of London, 1766, 49mm. diam. $3,150 £1,400

Gold hunting cased pocket chronometer by Brillman & Co., London, 1863, 52.5mm. diam. $3,375 £1,500

Silver repousse cased calendar verge watch, signed Langin, London, circa 1730, 54mm. diam. $3,600 £1,600

17th century watch movement by Henry Harper, 51mm. diam. $3,600 £1,600

Gold and enamel verge watch signed Breguet a Paris, 46mm. diam., circa 1790. $3,600 £1,600

Gold and enamel quarter repeating cylinder watch, by Francis Perigal, London, 48mm. diam. $3,825 £1,700

Late 18th century gilt metal pair cased striking cylinder chaise watch by Marriott, London, 132mm. diam. $3,825 £1,700

Rare tourbillon watch by Charles Frodsham, London, 1907. $3,940 £1,750

Repousse gold pair cased verge watch by Archambo of London, 1731, 48mm. diam. $4,050 £1,800

119

Silver verge pendulum watch by David Plumbe, London, circa 1710, 58mm. diam. $4,275 £1,900

Silver pair cased chronometer watch, signed Jessop, Southampton Street, Strand, London, No. 1972, 61mm. diam. $4,275 £1,900

Silver pair cased false pendulum verge watch, signed Wm. Harrison, London, 60mm. diam. $4,500 £2,000

Gold and enamel pair cased verge watch by George Prior, London, 1815, 51mm. diam. $4,500 £2,000

Silver cased full plate pocket chronometer by Robt. Molyneux, hallmarked 1839, 57mm. diam. $4,500 £2,000

Swiss gold quarter repeating Jacquemart verge watch, 56mm. diam. $4,725 £2,100

Gold pair cased repeating cylinder watch by Joseph Bosley, London, 18th century, 56mm. diam. $4,950 £2,200

Gold half hunting cased minute repeating keyless lever watch by Russells Ltd., Liverpool, 1900. $5,625 £2,500

Oval silver watch for the Turkish Market, with Turkish numerals and subsidiary lunar dial, 63mm. long. $5,625 £2,500

Mid 18th century silver pair cased verge watch by Markwick of London, 73mm. diam.
$5,625 £2,500

Early French silver verge watch by Estienne Hubert, Rouen, 54mm. diam.
$6,075 £2,700

Gold pair cased pocket chronometer by Thom. Earnshaw, 1801, 56mm. diam. $6,075 £2,700

Gold pair cased verge clock-watch by John Everell, London, 56mm. diam.
$6,300 £2,800

Gold half hunting cased keyless lever Karrusel, 1911, 52mm. diam.
$6,750 £3,000

Gold quarter repeating verge watch by Daniel Quare, circa 1720, 54mm. diam. $7,315 £3,250

Gold and pearl set verge watch, in the form of a basket, by Chevalier & Cochet, circa 1800, 34mm. long. $7,650 £3,400

Gold and tortoiseshell pair cased verge watch by David Lestourgeon, London, 1694, 52mm. diam.
$8,100 £3,600

Gold hunter cased minute repeating keyless lever watch, signed Hamilton & Inches, No. 30046, 55mm. diam. $8,550 £3,800

Lever watch by Barraud & Lunds. $9,000 £4,000

Gold hunting cased five minute repeating keyless lever watch by J. Alfred Jurgensen, Copenhagen, 54mm. diam. $9,450 £4,200

Gold pair cased pocket chronometer by Thos. Earnshaw, London, 58mm. diam. $9,450 £4,200

Gold and enamel duplex watch, signed Ilbery, London, 60mm. diam. $10,800 £4,800

17th century verge watch by Joseph Chamberlain, Norwich, 52mm. diam. $11,250 £5,000

Rare gold watch, signed Robt. Roskell, 56mm. diam. $12,150 £5,400

Huaut enamel verge watch, signed Huaut , A. Son A. E., 44mm. diam. $13,500 £6,000

Keyless wind watch by Charles Frodsham, London, 1888. $19,125 £8,500

Early 19th century gold and enamel quarter repeating musical watch for the Chinese market by Bovet, 64mm. diam. $19,125 £8,500

Early 19th century gold and enamel centre-seconds duplex watch for the Chinese market by Ilbery of London, 69mm. diam.
$29,250 £13,000

Mid 18th century rare musical striking quarter repeating chaise watch by J. Martineau, Snr., London, 145mm. diam.
$47,250 £21,000

19th century gold cased two-barrel lever watch by Breguet, 52mm. diam.
$56,250 £25,000

Watch by J. Norris, Amsterdam, in enamelled gold case, late 17th century, 3.9cm. diam.
$56,250 £25,000

Early 17th century silver and gilt metal cruciform watch by Abraham Cusins, 45mm. diam.
$94,500 £42,000

Early 17th century gold and enamel pair cased gold watch by Charles Bobinet, 1½in. diam.
$99,000 £44,000

Watch by Wm. Anthony with blue enamel back set with pearls and diamonds, circa 1810, 3½in. high.
$162,000 £72,000

Engraved silver gilt skull watch with silver crucifix, late 18th or early 19th century, 77mm. long.
$180,000 £80,000

Double-sided astronomical gold watch, inscribed J. W. Benson, London, circa 1870.
$276,430 £122,857

INDEX